Jane Shirreff, Mary Anne Shirreff

The music of Pizarro

Collection of sheet music from the late 18th and early 19th centuries

Jane Shirreff, Mary Anne Shirreff

The music of Pizarro

Collection of sheet music from the late 18th and early 19th centuries

ISBN/EAN: 9783742802385

Manufactured in Europe, USA, Canada, Australia, Japa

Cover: Foto ©Angelika Wolter / pixelio.de

Manufactured and distributed by brebook publishing software (www.brebook.com)

Jane Shirreff, Mary Anne Shirreff

The music of Pizarro

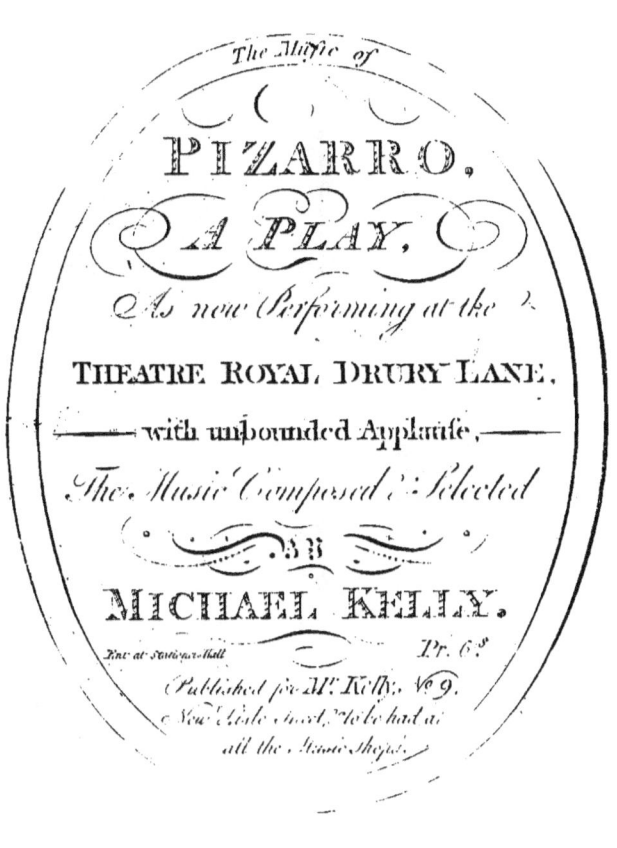

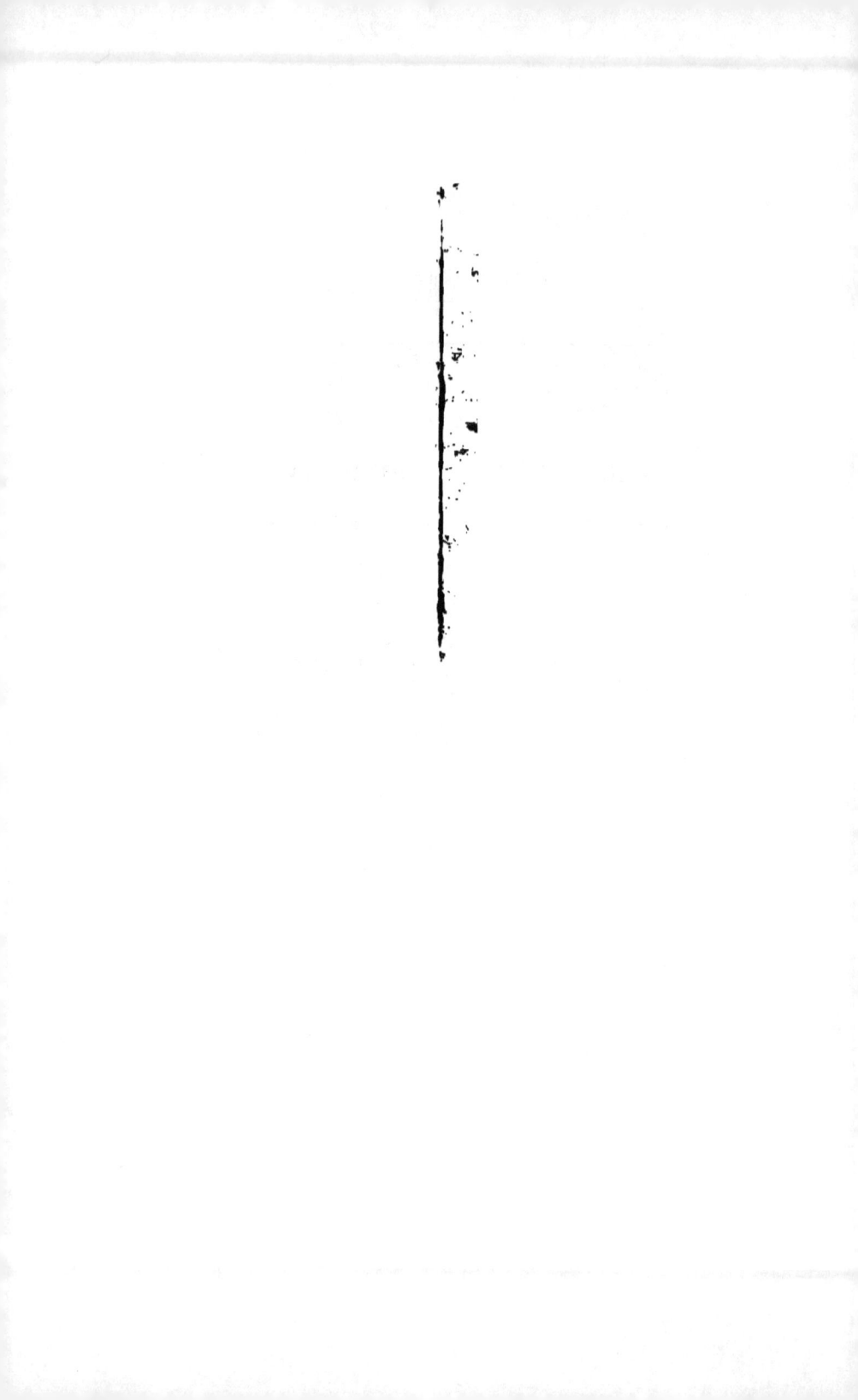

MARCH
Of Priests and Priestesses in the Temple of the Sun.

Gluck

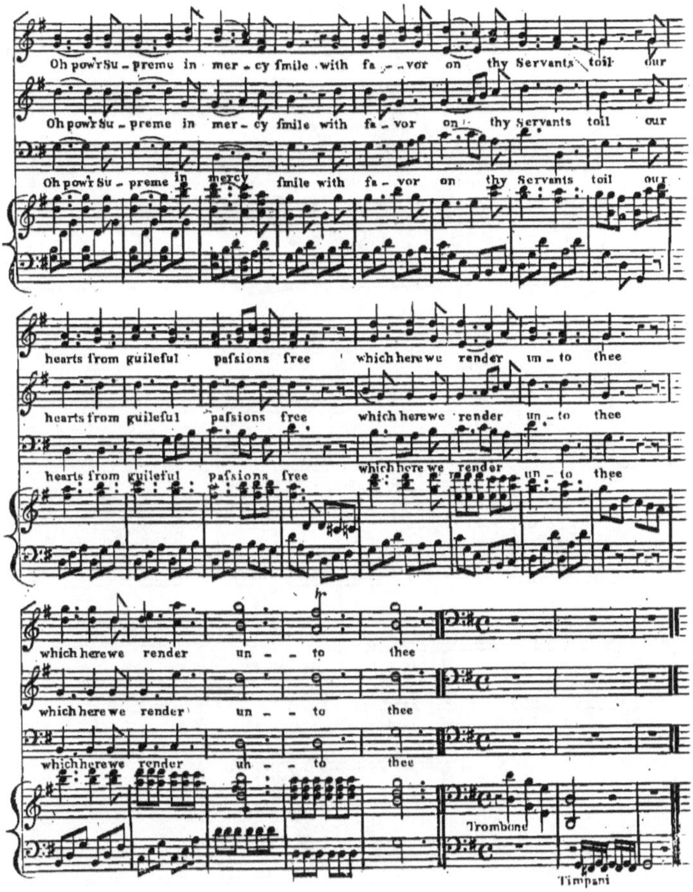
Oh pow'r Su _ preme in mer _ cy fmile with fa _ _ vor on thy Servants toil our
Oh pow'r Su _ preme in mer _ cy fmile with fa _ vor on thy Servants toil our
Oh pow'r Su _ preme in mercy fmile with fa _ vor on thy Servants toil our
hearts from guileful pafsions free which here we render un _ to thee
hearts from guileful pafsions free which here we render un _ to thee
hearts from guileful pafsions free which here we render un _ to thee
which here we render un _ _ to thee
which here we render un _ _ to thee
which here we render un _ _ to thee
Trombone
Timpani

CHORUS OF PRIESTS AND PRIESTESSES in the Temple of the Sun.

Sacchini

MARCH

Shaw

Allegro con Spirito

DISTANT MILITARY MARCH and CHORUS OF PERUVIANS.

Kelly

Yes be merciless thou Tempest dire.
Sung by Mrs Jordan.
Written by R. B. SHERIDAN, Esqr.

Now softly sunk the setting Sun
Beneath his wat'ry bed
The Ev'ning Watch was hush'd & done
The Pilot hung his head;

On the deck ROSA staid
To watch the waters glide,
Ah! no, ROSA no!
Such thought ne'er touch'd the Maid
'Twas HENRY by her side.

2

Night came and, now eight bells had rung,
While careless Sailors, ever cheary,
On the mid watch so jovial sung,
With tempers labour cannot weary;

I, little to their mirth inclined,
While tender thoughts rushed on my fancy,
And my warm sighs increased the wind,
Looked on the moon, and thought of Nancy.

3

And now arrived that jovial night
When every true bred tar carrouses,
When, o'er the grog, all hands delight
To toast their sweethearts and their spouses;

Round went the can, the jest the glee,
While tender wishes filled each fancy
And when, in turn, it came to me,
I, heaved a sigh, and toasted Nancy

4

Next morn a storm came on at four,
At six, the elements in motion
Plunged me and three poor Sailors more
Headlong within the foaming ocean;

Poor wretches! they soon found their graves,
For me, it may be only fancy,
But love seemed to forbid the waves
To snatch me from the arms of Nancy.

5

Scarce the foul hurricane was cleared,
Scarce winds and waves had ceased to rattle,
When a bold Enemy appeared,
And, dauntless, we prepared for battle:

And now, while some loved friend or wife,
Like lightning, rushed on every fancy;
To providence I trusted life,
Put up a prayer, and thought on Nancy

6

At last twas in the month of may,
The crew, it being lovely weather,
At three, A. M. discovered day
And England's chalky cliffs together;

At seven up channel how we bore
While hopes and fears rushed on my fancy,
At twelve I gaily jumped ashore
And to my throbbing heart pressed Nancy.

For two Flutes.

2

Honour abhors the darksome Cell
Unbless'd by Gratitudes bright flame
There pale distrust and treach'ry dwell
There fraud asserts her wily claim
Oft be my fervent vows renew'd
At the shrine of Gratitude.

2

Had Fate from its bounty propitiously lent,
Enough but to furnish the Cot of content,
The dictates of Love in that Cot I'd pursue,
For the Friend of my heart would partake of it too.

3

But Nancy with nought but her truth, to endear,
With nothing to give to distress, but a tear,
Can ne'er look for comfort with ruin in view,
And the Friend of her heart to partake of it too.

A CATALOGUE of the FAVORITE OPERAS
with the OVERTURES & SONGS, &c. Extracted; as Composed & Selected by STEPHEN STORACE

London, Printed for & Sold by J. Dale, Music Seller, N° 19 Cornhill, & the corner of Bolton Street Piccadilly

THE CHEROKEE
Overture to Do.	1.6
High disdaining	1.
Seventh Night	1.
Sweet Sympathy	1.
The Lord of Lords	1.
Sons of Valor, loud laughing	1.
Ah, how can I bid her Adieu	1.
Our Country's our Ship do, do	1.
Oh hail the King, Coo	1.
And the joyful Lambkin (Duet)	1.
To Honor's fame the silent Tomb to	1.
The Chorus of British Marksmen	6

THE PRIZE or 2.5.3.8.
The Lise Plant &c	1.
He loves me (Duet)	1.
From my bud good chin to.	1.
Never Happy at all	1.

THE GLORIOUS 1st of JUNE
Overture to Do.	1.
O dry my Tears	1.
No live but to Conquer, Song with Sym.	1.
Thou in War or the Chair	1.
The Line was formed	1.
O'er the vast Surging of the Deep	1.
When tis Night or the Mid watch	1.
Soon to the Village Delights	1.
Sur Fives adopted by Sea or	1.

LODOISKA
The Overture, to a Sub is called the Alarch &	1.
Symphonies to the 2.3.5. Acts ... allso Four	1.
NEW additional Numbers Symphonies as will be	1.
given gratis to those who will purchase the	1.
Overture as printed by Preal	1.
Ah! Lodoiska	1.
Ye streams that round my Prison Creep	1.
When the dark and Midnight	1.
When we Flourish	1.
Sweet Bird that cheers	1.
Hark Hark the Magic	1.
Pleasant was Waving Wood	1.
Florella the her Eyes (Trio)	1.6

MY GRANDMOTHER
Overture to Do.	1.
So in gay an Opening Rose	1.
Vintagers do	1.
Well a Day Lackaday	1.
Cristal Fair	1.
The Masquerade Song	1.
Never think of Love	1.
The Return Song Say how can Words do	1.

THE SIEGE of BELGRADE
Overture to Do.	1.
The Favorite March piano Do.	1.
The Mamaluke Song by Storace	1.
Shall Wait the Serum Fate	1.
Plate in the Door in May	1.
No more I'll brave the tender Night	1.
Saw him up toward a Wife	1.
How fair know how to reward Love	1.
Te Bow is the Battle	1.
The Sapling Oak	1.
of Plighted Faith (Duet)	1.6
Then we think by this to coax me (Trio)	1.6
Tis mighty fine	1.
Is plaited in verse Day service	1.
How far know how to take you (Duet)	1.

THE PIRATES
Overture to Do.	1.6
The Favorite Dance in Do.	1.
Lullaby	1.
No more his Peace charming	1.
Love who listen	1.
As wrapt in Sleep	1.
In Childhood's week is happy Day	1.
There the Silvered Waters Roam	1.
The Indian Pow... (Duet)	1.
My vicious Spirits	1.
Oh the Pretty Creature	1.
Sweet little twinkling little explorer	1.
The Magic Lambkin	1.

THE THREE & TWICE
Overture to Do.	1.6
Ca, ai, my Love	1.
Little Taffline	1.
Palsied Pa's simple Cotton Sock	1.
I'll bid my Trembling Heart	1.
Oh hush er that grew in Cottage way	1.
Around the Old Oak (Trio)	1.6
Full many a lad in lak us to Say	1.

MAHMOUD & the IRON CHEST
The Favorite Dance in one Book	1.5
Overture to Mahmoud	2.
Where Ladies Men or Slaves	1.
The Woodman Sent the Jovial Cry	1.
Tell Tell the Bell	1.
Oh happy, Yo Youth	1.
From Shades of Night	1.
Sigh in the Wind (Duet)	1.
The Carpet Weaver	1.

From the IRON CHEST
Overture to Do.	1.6
Sweet Little Barbara (Duet)	1.
Down the dept at a Widow's Gate	1.
Down by the River that grows a green willow	1.

MISCELLANEOUS ARTICLES BY STORACE
O Steal to the Harp in Train of Tempte	1.
See One Piece of Rose Leaves	1.
Captivity a favorite Song	1.
Lamentation of the Queen of France (to)	1.
Care Donna an Italian Song	1.
To man can (Trio)	2.6
Six Sonatinas for the Piano Forte with I'm lost or for Captain missing	3.

OPERAS adapted for the FLUTE
The Cherokee	1.
The Prize	1.6
The Glorious First of June	1.
Lodoiska	1.
My Grandmother	1.
The Siege of Belgrade	1.
The Pirates	1.
The Three & the Deuce	1.6
Mahmoud	1.
The Iron Chest	1.6

FOR THE GUITAR
The Siege of Belgrade	3.
The Pirates	3.
The Prize	3.

NB. The above Works are the sole Property of Dale & Entered at Stationers Hall. The Public are respectfully entreated to take Notice that each Piece in future will be marked & that Catalogue, with his address is shown — to prevent spurious Copies, as many of the above have been Pirated & sold, Scarcely to Sell or if Sung in above Operas.

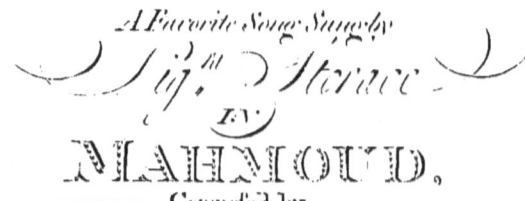

Never, he told her, he would be a rover,
She fondly thought he told her true
But how shall the Maid his truth discover
Ah will he plight his vows anew.

If never, never her voice deceiv'd him,
Now while telling of loves long ago
Can he forget the girl, who believ'd him,
Down in the vale where violets grow.

London. Printed & Sold by L. LAVENU, Music Seller to His Royal High.ss the Prince of Wales, N.º 29 New Bond Street.

THE WHITE MAN,

A favorite Ballad,

The Words taken from

Mr. PARK'S, Travels,

and Set to Music, with an Accompaniment

for the

HARP or PIANO FORTE,

by

Miss Abrams.

Ent. at Stationers Hall.

Pr. 1ˢ 6

"He found the Inhabitants of the Village either averse, or afraid, to give him lodging, or entertainment; and having turned his horse loose, he sought Shelter, from a Storm of thunder & rain, under a tree. At length, as night approached that kindness & humanity inherent in the female Sex, to which he had often been indebted on former occasions, came to his relief on the present.— A Poor Negro Woman, returning from the labours of the field, observed that he was wet, weary & dejected, and taking up his Saddle & Bridle, told him to follow her. She led him to her Cottage, lighted up a lamp, procured him an excellent Supper of fish, & plenty of Corn for his horse; after which, she spread a Mat upon the floor, and said he might remain there for the night. For this well timed bounty, our traveller presented her with two of the Four brass buttons Which remained on his Waistcoat."

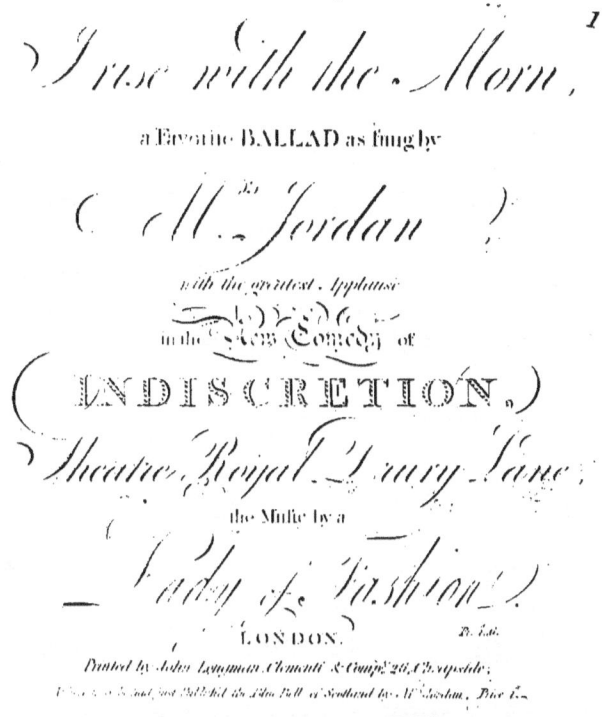

(2)

Alas! my poor heart, once so sprightly and gay
No more can I boast to be free
Love's fever consumes it — Ah! fatal the day
That brought such a torment to me!

At Night my sad Pillow's bedew'd with my tears
Sleep flies till entomb'd I shall be
In the Grave there's an end to troubles and
And that's consolation for me.

A prey to tender anguish

A favorite Song

with an Accompaniment

for the

PIANO FORTE

Composed by

Dr. HAYDN.

Entered at Stationer's Hall.　　　　　　　　Price 1s.

LONDON

Printed by Longman, Clementi & Co. 26 Cheapside

Larghetto

A prey to ten—der an—guish, of ev'ry joy be—reav'd, How oft I sigh and lan—guish, How

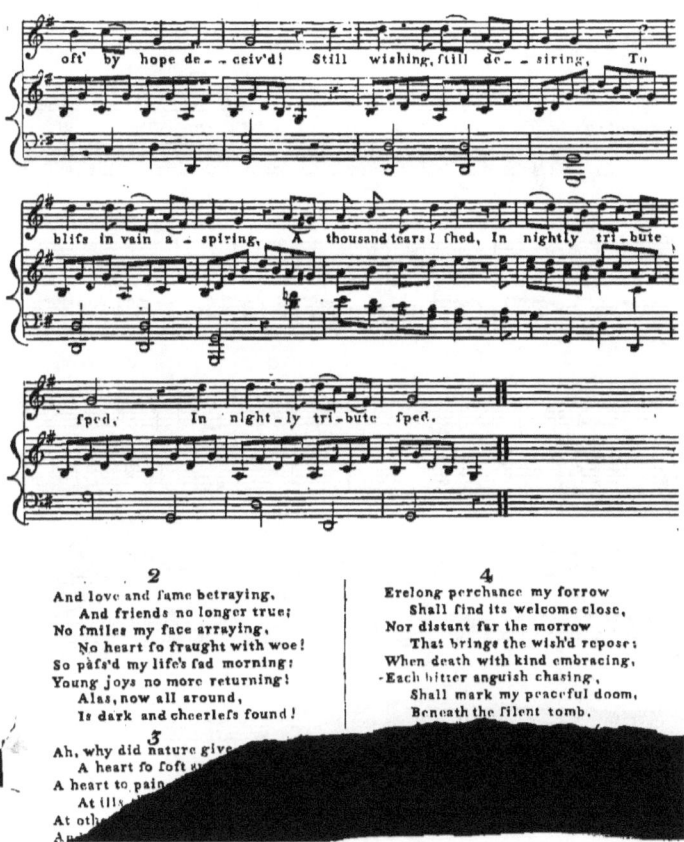

2
And love and fame betraying,
   And friends no longer true;
No smiles my face arraying,
   No heart so fraught with woe!
So pass'd my life's sad morning;
Young joys no more returning!
   Alas, now all around,
   Is dark and cheerless found!

3
Ah, why did nature give
   A heart so soft
A heart to pain
   At ills
At oth
An

4
Erelong perchance my sorrow
   Shall find its welcome close,
Nor distant far the morrow
   That brings the wish'd repose;
When death with kind embracing,
-Each bitter anguish chasing,
   Shall mark my peaceful doom,
   Beneath the silent tomb.

The Confession

A Favorite CANZONET
with an Accompaniment for a
HARP or PIANO FORTE,
the Music by
An AMATEUR.

Pr. 1ˢ

L O N D O N.

Printed & Sold at Bland & Weller's, Music Warehouse, 23 Oxford Street.

Lento — With sor--row and re--pentance true Fa--ther I

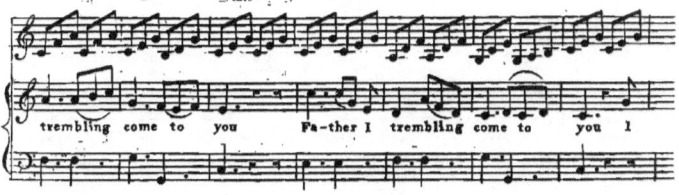

trembling come to you Fa--ther I trembling come to you I

2
Oh rev'rend Father if you knew'
The charms of him alas untrue;
Oh had you heard the false one swear,
I was the fairest of the Fair,
You would not Holy Sir refuse;
So slight a weakness to excuse;
He swore he'd never love me lefs,
Oh Father must I then confefs.

3
To grief eternal grief a prey
His name is all my heart can say
When bathed in sad repentant tears
Still to my mind his name appears
Yes tis that name that name alone
Which bends me now before thy throne
ALCANDOR — but I cant exprefs
Oh Father must I then confefs

4
Oh tell him should he come to you,
And thus like me for mercy sue
Tell him of all the crimes accurst
Tell him Inconstancys the worst
Tell him that he who's false in love
Can ne'er hope Pity from above
Tell him that I alone can blefs
And send him to me to confefs.

GERMAN FLUTE

2

Philomel down in the Grove broke sweetly the silence of Night O I wish that the tear drop would flow but felt too much anguish to weep till warm with the weight of my woe I sunk on my pillow to sleep to

Poco f

Me thoughts that my Love, as I lay,
His ringlets all clotted with gore,
In the paleness of Death, seem'd to say,
Alas! we must never meet more!
Yes, yes, my belov'd we must part,
The steel of my Rival was true;
The Assassin has struck on that heart,
Which beat with such fervour for you.

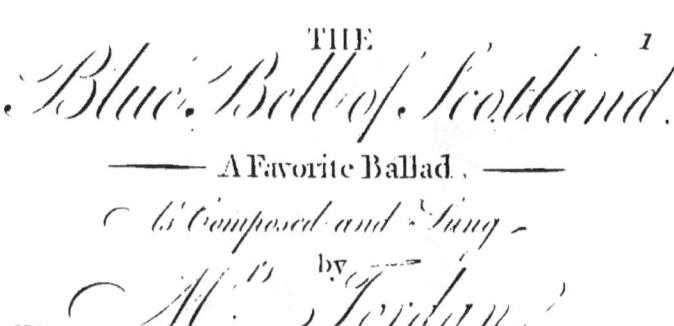

THE
Blue Bell of Scotland.
—— A Favorite Ballad ——
Is Composed and Sung
by
Mrs Jordan
at the
THEATRE ROYAL DRURY LANE.

London, Printed & Sold by John Longman, Clementi, & Co 26 Cheapside.

Andante

Oh! where and oh where is your Highland Laddie gone, Oh! where and oh where is your Highland Laddie gone;

2

Oh where and oh where did your Highland Laddie dwell
He dwelt in merry Scotland at the sign of the Blue bell
And its oh in my heart I love my Laddie well.

3

In what Cloaths in what Cloaths is your Highland Laddie clad
His Bonnet of the Saxon green and his Waiscoat of the Plaid
And its oh in my heart I love my Highland Lad.

4

Suppose and suppose that your Highland Lad should die
The Bagpipes should play over him and I'd sit me down and cry
And Its oh in my heart I wish he may not die.

N.B. The *Guitar* to be play'd as it stands, but to be sung an Octave lower.

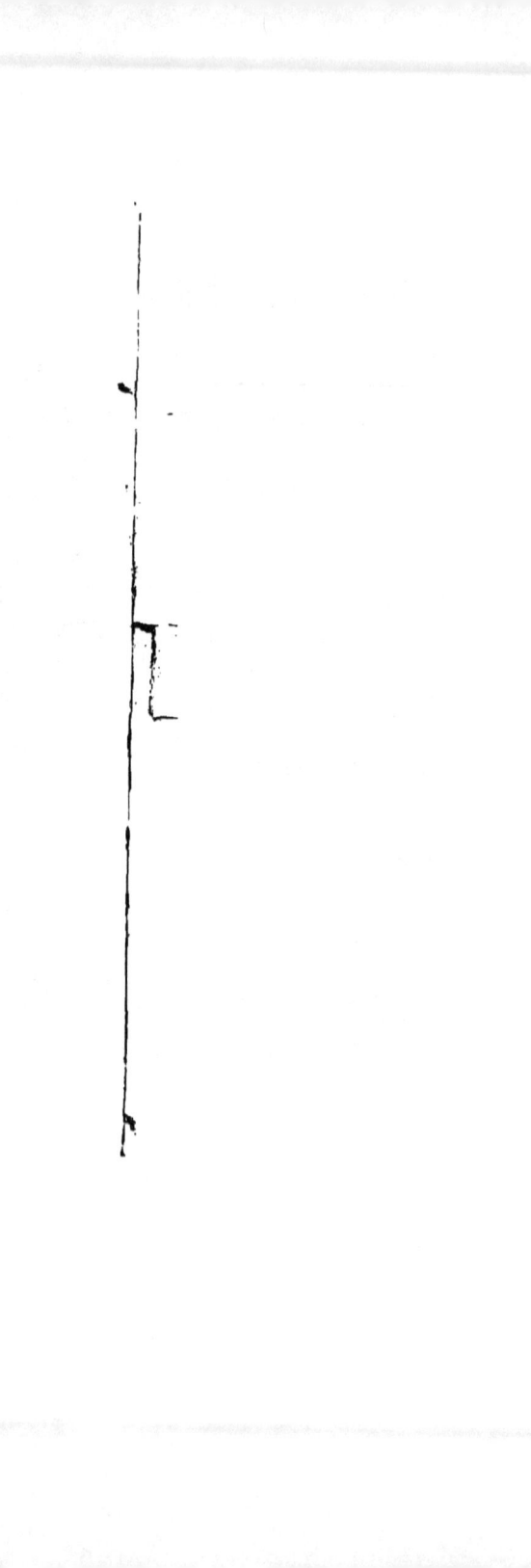

SOFT MUSIC LET MY HUMBLE LAY,

Sung by Miss Farren,

—— in the ——

New Comedy of False Colours,

Composed by

Mr SUETT.

LONDON. Price 1s

Printed & Sold by Preston & Son, at their Wholesale Warehouses 97 Strand.

Soft Music, let my humble lay, Thy sweetest accents move, Soft Music, let my humble lay, Thy

2.
That when to court the willing Strain
She tunes her graceful Art,
Each trembling Tone may breathe again
The Sigh that rends my Heart.

3.
And should thy plaintive murmurs steal
A symphathetic Tear,
In fond emotion then reveal
ANTONIO sent thee here.

2	3
For love deserted, broken vows, / Of false and perjur'd Man; / She did the fickle God accuse, / Which could her heart trepan: / The dusky night began to draw / It's influence o'er the main; / She starts, she looks, she surely saw, / The Ghost of CRAZY JANE.	Now trembling at the aweful scene, / She saw the Spectre move; / And gently gliding o'er the green, / Soon lost it in the grove: / There wand'ring 'midst the lonely wood, / With sadness in her train; / Is often seen in direful mood, / The Ghost of CRAZY JANE.

For the Guitar

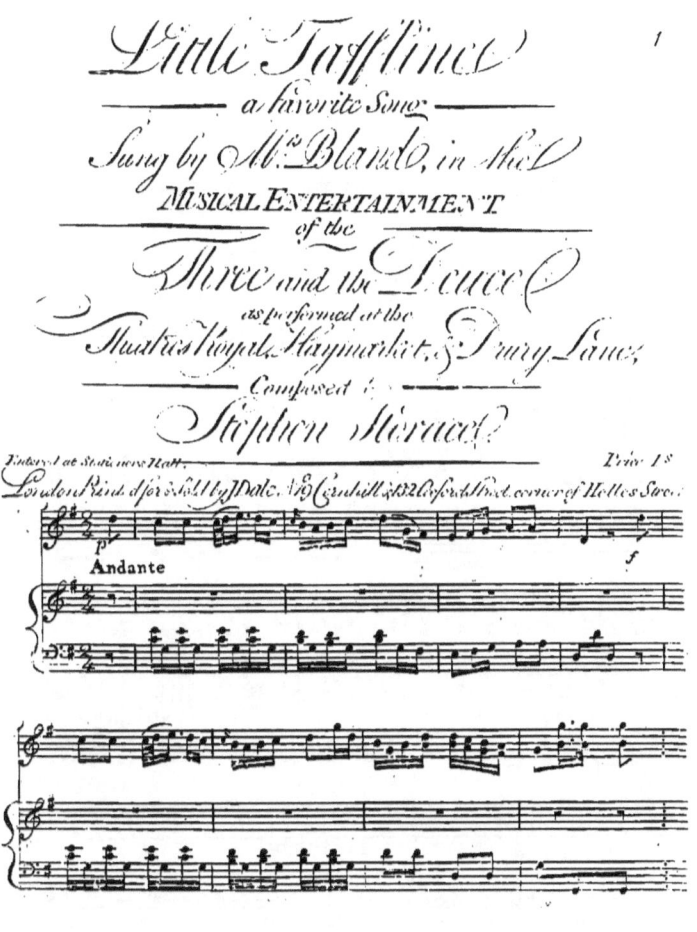

Oh! then what pleasure to be seen,
When the Lads at evening meet!
With silken sash of pink or green,
Silken roses on my feet!
How folks will stare,
As hir goes by,
"See see they'll cry,
Her flanty air!
And the Lads will say "Dear heart what a flash!
Look at little Taffline with a silken sash!

The Billet Doux

A FAVOURITE BALLAD.

Sung by Mr. Harrison at
MESS.rs HARRISON & KNYVETT'S VOCAL CONCERTS.

Written by J. O'Keefe, Esq.r

COMPOSED BY Mr. SHIELD.

Price 1.s

LONDON:
Printed for Harrison & C.o N.o 78 Fleet Street.

The Billet-doux when I recieve,
I press it to my throbbing heart;
Sweet words! I cry, such joys you give,
Oh! never, never thence depart.
And now it to my Lips is press'd;
But when the magic name I view,
Again I clasp it to my breast,
My fond, my tender Billet-doux.

London Printed & Sold by L. LAVENU, Music Seller to His
Royal Highness the Prince of Wales, 29 New Bond Street

THE ORPHANS PRAYER,

A Pathetic Ballad,

THE WORDS BY

M. G. Lewis, Esqr.

—— and Set to Music ——

with an Accompaniment for the

Harp or Piano Forte,

BY

MISS ABRAMS.

Ent. at Stationers Hall   Pr. 1/6

N.B. in Order that no Printer or Publisher may plead Ignorance they are
desired to take Notice, that the Words & Music of this Song is Property.

L. Lavc

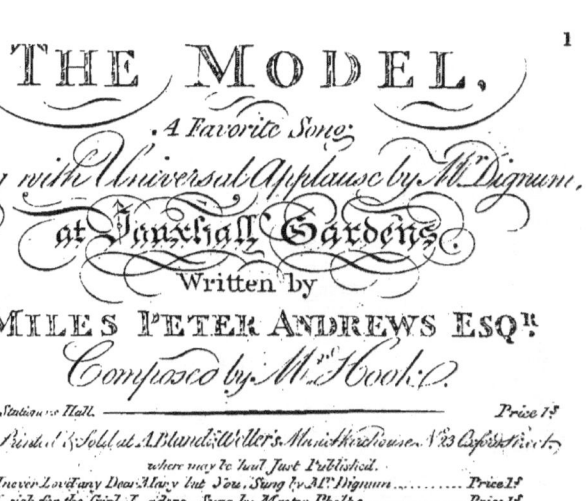

THE MODEL,

A Favorite Song;

Sung with Universal Applause by Mr Dignum,

at Vauxhall Gardens.

Written by

MILES PETER ANDREWS ESQR.

Composed by Mr Hook.

2

His Heart is Enlarg'd, tho' his Income is Scant,
He lessens his little for others that want,
Tho' his Children's dear claims on his Industry prefs,
He has something to spare for the Child of distrefs,
    He seeks no Idle squabble,
    He joins no thoughtlefs rabble,
      To clear his way,
      From day to day,
    His honest views extend,
    When he speaks 'tis verily,
    When he smiles 'tis merrily,
Dear to him his sport, his Toil, his Honour and his Friend.

3

How charming to find in his humble retreat,
That bliss so much sought, so unknown to the great,
The Wife only anxious her fondness to prove,
The playfull Endearments of infantine love,
    Relaxing from his labours,
    Amid his welcome Neighbours,
      With plain regale,
      With jest and tale,
    The happy Hero, see,
    No vain schemes confounding him,
    All his joys surrounding him,
Dear he holds, his Native land, its Laws, and Liberty.

Chearful see yon Shepherd Boy
Climbing up the craggy rocks,
As he views the dappled Sky,
Pleas'd the Cuckoo's note he mocks;
 Cuckoo! Cuckoo! Cuckoo! Cuckoo!
Pleas'd the Cuckoo's note he mocks.
Now advancing o'er the plain,

Evening's dusky shades appear,
And the Cuckoo's voice again,
Softly steals upon mine ear,
While retireing from the view,
Thus she bids the Day adieu;
 Cuckoo! Cuckoo! Cuckoo! Cuckoo!
Thus she bids the Day adieu.

4

3d Verse

The Devil among the Taylors.

A Favorite Dance.

Arranged as a Rondo, for the Piano Forte.

Pr 1s. 6

London, Printed by John Longman, Clementi, & Co. 26, Cheapside

A CATALOGUE of the FAVORITE OPERAS

with the OVERTURES & SONGS &c. Extracted, as
Composed & Selected
by
STEPHEN STORACE.

London, Printed for & Sold by J. Dale Music Seller, 19 Cornhill, & the corner of Holles Street Oxford Street.

THE CHEROKEE

Overture to D^o	1.6
Bitter tho' dissembling	1.–
Save as I could, Night	1.–
Sweet Nymphalin	1.–
A Sailor lov'd a Lass	1.–
Dream'd I not the Spark ling	1.–
A Shepherd was that heart mine	1.–
Our Country Is our Ship &c. &c.	1.–
In what is ride the buoy Vary	1.–
And she enjoin'd Paulina (Duet)	1.–
In Vienna Town the oth of Eighth	1.–
The Cherokee Brides Martha's	1.–

The PRIZE or 2.5.3.8.

The Rose that's	1.–
Meet me by Softly (Duet)	1.–
From my little rock I'm	1.–
O'er the Delightful still	1.–

THE GLORIOUS 1st of JUNE

Overture to D^o	
Come my Love	1.–
He lives but to Conquer, & longs to be Sure	1.–
When in War on the Ocean	1.–
The Time was Prized	1.–
O'er the wide surges of the Deep	1.–
When the Bullet is the Mid watch	.6
Sheen to the Village Delights	1.–
Five Tunes, Adapted for Stores	

LODOISKA 8.0

The Overture Scotch is called the Minuet &	
Sunfits in the 2nd & 3rd Acts — Also the	
Still celebrated Marches, Songs &c. a will be	
given gratis to those who will purchase the	
Overture as printed by Dale	
Melodists	
Ye streams that round my Prison Creep	1.–
When the chords tied Midnight	1.–
When my Flora's	1.–
Sweet Bird that sweet	1.–
Hark Hark the Music	1.–
I heard some Warning sigh	1.–
Flow'd it in her Voice (Trio)	1.6

MY GRANDMOTHER

Overture to D^o	1.–
In setting or Opening Recces	1.–
Tidely Toppy	1.–
When a Boy like a Page	1.–
Good Lack	1.–
The Masquerade Song	1.–
Never think of Love	1.–
The Pictur Song so twas on Monday	1.–

THE SIEGE of BELGRADE 10.6

Overture to D^o	2.6
The Favorite March from D^o	.6
The Minuet & Air Sung by Storace	.6
Ah will Hail the Serene Day	1.–
Pibita is the Home in May	1.–
Seymor I'll have the kind o Sigh	1.–
Some him oys I smoor'd a Wife	1.–
Five fine from how'to relish Toys	1.–
The Rose & the Lilly	1.–
The Sapling Oak	1.–
O Plighted Faith (Duet)	1.–
The you think he this to o'er an D^o	1.–
Tis mighty Love	1.–
My plaint to no one Ever moves	1.–
Hear the Thais Imme & lik you Duet	1.–

THE PIRATES 12.6

Overture to D^o	1.–
The Favorite Duett sen D^o	1.–
Lullaby	1.–
No more has Peace charming	1.–
Lovers who Listen	1.–
In courapt in Sleep	1.–
In Childhood's morn 'tis happy Days	1.–
When the Solemn Watch is Begun	1.–
The Indian Poor (Duet)	1.–
My rising Spirits	1.–
Oh the Pretty Creature	1.–
Compleat the winding Path explore	1.–
The Magic Lantern	1.–

THE THREE & the DEUCE 8.0

Overture to D^o	1.6
Go not my Love	1.–
Little Taffline	1.–
Behold the sample Village Toys	1.–
Oh bid not Trembling Heart	1.–
O'er hanks that grew in Killarney	1.–
Around the old Oak (Glee)	1.–
Full many a Lad in Dowel's Vale	.6

MAHMOUD & the IRON CHEST

The Favorite Over over in an Back	1.6
Overture to Mahmoud	1.–
When I choose More or Shiver	1.–
The Measure Say II the kindest Ore	1.–
Tell I I the Small	1.–
A hopeless Exile	1.–
From Buds of Night	1.–
Say in the Wind (Duet)	1.–
The Captive Beaver	1.–

From the IRON CHEST

Overture to D^o	1.6
Five times by the Taper (Glee)	1.6
Sweet Little Barbara (Duet)	1.–
Minna thro slept at a Widow's tale	1.–
Down by the River thro grows a great willow	1.–

MISCELLANEOUS ARTICLES BY STORACE

Captive the Harp in Praise of Bought	1.–
Sir Ow, Two or Three Voice	
Captivity a favorite Song	1.–
Lamentation of the Queen of France D^o	1.2
Care Donna an Italian Song	2.6
In no som D^o	
Six Sonatinas for the Piano Forte with Preludes in Beginners Improved	3.–

OPERAS adapted for the FLUTE

The Cherokee	3.–
The Prize	1.6
The Glorious First of June	1.6
Lodoiska	2.–
My Grandmother	1.6
The Siege of Belgrade	2.–
The Pirates	2.6
The Three & the Deuce	2.6
Mahmoud	
The Iron Chest	2.6

FOR THE GUITAR

The Siege of Belgrade	3.–
The Pirates	
The Prize	

N.B. The above Works as they are Reprints of HAVE Entered at Stationers Hall The Public are respectfully entreated to take Notice that to each Piece in future will be added this Catalogue with his address as above — to prevent spurious editions as many of the New ones have been Imitated & will otherwise Sold as if Songs in & above Operas.

Since first he fled,
The life I've led,
  Has been a life of pain;
Some jeer'd me fair,
A' cried me mair
  Will he return again.

Mr. NEWBOUND.
Ne'er mind their crack,
Now, I'm come back,
  Let inward pining cease:
My folly past
May be the last,
  That e'er will break your peace.

DUETT Sung By M^{RS} SUTHERLAND and MR NEWBOUND. In the Scots Pastoral JAMIE and BESS or The LAIRD in Disguise.

MR NEWBOUND.
Sym. Were't not for Kate's too pow'rful charms, I lik'd the plaid and highland dress; But ev'ry thought of war and arms I gladly quit for

M^{RS} SUTHERLAND.
our embrace. O honey'd accents far too sweet, They like enchantment to me seem; My happiness is too complete Ah! Simon sure I only dream!

To what shall I my bliss compare!
In Simon I have ev'ry wish —
   MR NEWBOUND.
Then, in your bliss let Simon share,
And make him happy with a kiss.
   M^{RS} SUTHERLAND.
If kisses gi'e him such relief,
I have a treasure for his sake,
And never need he taste of grief,
Since, at discretion, he may take.
   MR NEWBOUND.
Far hence be ilk intruding care,
While, thus, I press thee to my breast;
Ten thousand sweets ye have to spare,
And ane to me, my Kate's a feast.

   M^{RS} SUTHERLAND.
Such kisses as I thus bestow,
I only to my Simon len';
When sweeter on his lips they grow,
He'll, kindly, pay them back again.
   MR NEWBOUND.
O never can those sweets increase,
Bestow'd like Nature's on the flow'rs;
For what ye think my lips possess,
My Katty, only flows frae your's.
   M^{RS} SUTHERLAND.
If freely gi'en, with loving heart,
They sweeter be, then, such are nine;
But never can my lips impart
A sweet not far excell'd by thine.

   BOTH.
Soon may the happy day appear,
When we may kiss, nor care wha ken't;
When greater bliss our hearts will share,
And we embrace without restraint.

Song Sung by
In the Scots Pastoral JAMIE and BESS or The Laird in Disguise.

It's my part to flight her, and his, sure, to right her,
And, as he best can, he may do it himsell:
I'd hae my throat nicket, ere I were sae tricket,
Or the warld, on me, gat sic stories to tell.

Had she constant prov'd, I still would have lov'd,
But, that it is otherwise, I'm nae to blame;
I scorn the Beauty, who kensna her duty,
And wishes to play me so cunning a game.

Tho' late, in his absence, I pin'd and lamented,
Now, he's safe return'd, my heart is contented;
The pleasure, I have in this day's happy meeting,
Repays me for a' my past sobbing and greeting.

Anes mair now, delighted, I view the green fields,
And taste a' the sweets which kind Nature still yields;
Nae langer sic beauties are irksome to me,
Altho' they remind me, dear Simon, of thee.

Flow on then, sweet river, your murmurs now please me,
Nae langer, in vain, will ye strive, now, to ease me;
Tho' late on your banks I sat sighing and mourning,
Nae mair now, I sigh for my Simon's returning.

Song Sung By Mrs HAMILTON.
In the Scots Pastoral JAMIE and BESS or The Laird in Disguise.

So warmly he press'd, that ere I was aware,
He slyly had stowen a kiss;
Yet, I fan my heart could not blame him so far,
As allow me to take it amiss.

His love, with such sweetness endearing, he told,
I heard his kind tale with content;
And thought it but vain to appear longer cold,
When I found my heart beating consent.

In his arms I fell, and with look of regard.
For I could be no longer unkind;
To Jamie my feelings I freely declar'd,
And honestly open'd my mind.

With rapture he heard the confession I made,
And swore he would love me thro' life; (glad,
And, with the sweet hope, my fond heart now is
That to Jamie I'll soon be a wife.

Song Sung By M^R. BIGGS.
In the Scots Pastoral JAMIE and BESS or The Laird in Disguise.

To slight she sweet a prize,
O what an ass is he!
I wad be far mair wise,
Cud she but think o' me.

Were she o' me as fain,
I'd nae be cauld nor shy;
He ne'er cud shaw disdain,
Gin he had lov'd as I.

Whene'er I speak of love, ye frown,
Bonny laſſie, &c.
And that pits a' my courage down;
My bonny lowland laſſie.

Gin ye ae kindly look wad wear,
Bonny laſſie, &c.
A' this gloom wad diſappear;
My bonny lowland laſſie.

But, gin ye dinna deign to ſmile,
Bonny laſſie, &c.
There's nonght, in life, that's worth my while;
My bonny lowland laſſie!

In Death's embrace, then only kind,
Bonny laſſie, &c.
I my reſt and peace maun find;
My bonny lowland laſſie!

Song Sung By Mr. TINGEY.
In the Scots Pastoral JAMIE and BESS or The Laird in Disguise.

How happy the youth, when to love he's in-clin'd, Who finds his dear fair, like my Bes-sy prove kind; So ex-treme is his joy, his plea-sure so great, Tho' I feel, I can't tell you how hap-py his state.

All description it baffles, no words can impart
One half of the bliss, which he feels in his heart;
Her consent obtain'd, such emotions arise,
He would burst, if they found not a vent at his eyes!

Song Sung By M^R. TINGEY.
In the Scots Paftoral JAMIE and BESS or The Laird in Difguife.

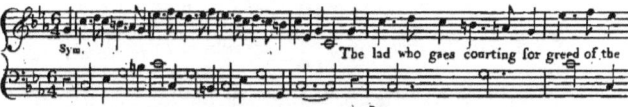

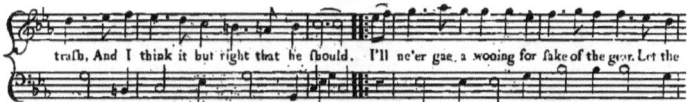
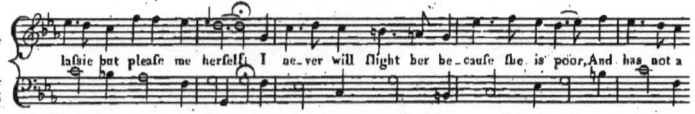

Nor will I e'er think it below me to wed,
When a lafs of true merit I find;
Nor care I farthing how humble the maid,
If fhe is but loving and kind.

Tho' proud-hearted Coxcombs may fay it is mean,
To marry beneath my degree;
I care not, by fuch, how my conduct is feen,
It is of no moment to me.

In choofing a darling companion for life,
For myfelf, I'm determin'd to judge;
And if I am pleas'd to make Befsy my wife,
Who elfe has a title to grudge?

Song Sung By Mrs NEWBOUND.

In the Scots Paſtoral JAMIE and BESS or The Laird in Diſguiſe.

Tho' Boreas lang may rudely blaw, And hill and dale be clad wi' fna', Yet gloomy winter wears a-wa, And joyfu' Spring appears. Then, Nature, ance mair, ſmiling, Ilk fil-ly fear be-guil-ing, With plenty, crowns the toil-ing of bu-ſy In-duſ-try. Sym.

Tho' lang ſhe's bow'd 'neath Fortune's blaſt,
My Beſſy will won up, at laſt,
My Beſſy, now, wons up, at laſt,
And happier days appear.

Soon, ſhall I ſee her ſmiling,
A' my paſt fears beguiling,
The thought repays my toiling,
For her, this mony day.

This night, I'll tell a ſtory,
Will make them blyth and ſorry,
Will make them blyth and ſorry,
At the ſtrange turns of Fate!

While hearing, they ſhall wonder,
And ca't a wyly blunder,
But, kent for truth, like thunder,
Will ſtrike them wi' amaze.

It, then, will be nae ſpring of wo!
'Cauſe he has wedded ane o'er low,
'Cauſe he has wedded ane o'er low,
And far beneath his rank.

Her, ſoon, his equal he ſhall ſee,
And, wi' the tale, delighted he
His heart and hand, content, ſhall gi'e,
And bliſs his happy fate.

And, when, in wedlock they are join'd,
May they ilk comfort in it find,
May they ilk comfort in it find,
Which e'er that ſtate could yield.

Love, wi' their days, increaſing,
Lang may they live, poſſeſſing,
Ilk joy, and earthly bliſſing,
Kind Heav'n can beſtow.

O Providence! now, hear me,
And, in the evening, cheer me,
And, in the evening, cheer me,
Of my declining age!

Thy Goodneſs, then, admiring,
To greater joys aſpiring,
I'll pleas'd, frae life, retiring,
Ly down amang the Dead!

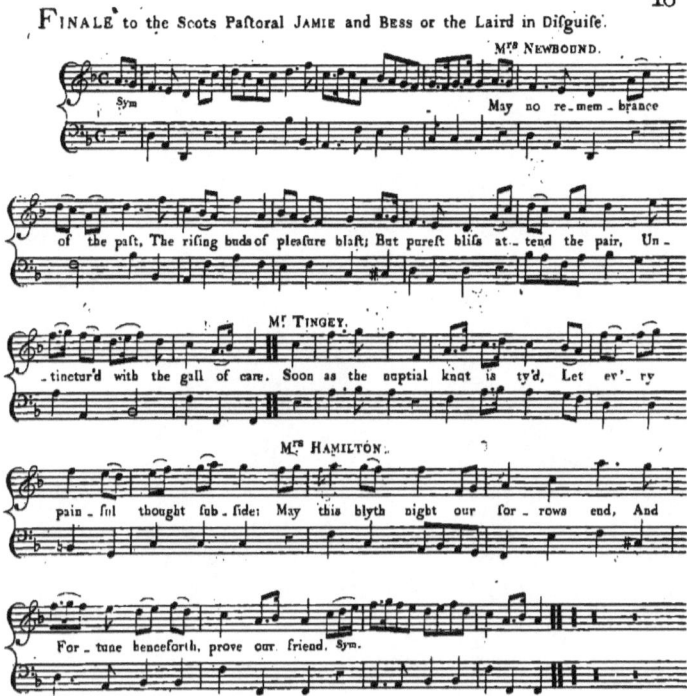

Mr. SUTHERLAND.
May ev'ry gen'rous lover find
His darling fair, like Betsy, kind;
And ever meet the due reward
Of an unfeign'd and pure regard.

First all the Female Voices, Piano. — Then Da. Capo Male and Female Voices, Forte.
What heart! but will, with rapture, join
To supplicate the Power Divine!
Which sends such blissings from above,
As the reward of gen'rous love.

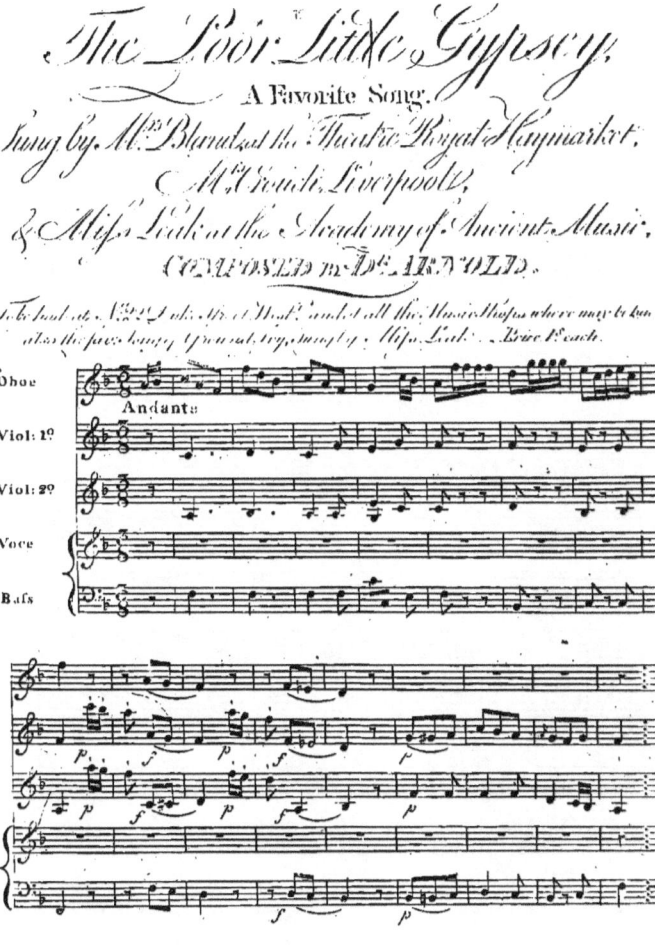

2

I fear from this line you have been a fad man,
And to harm us poor girls have form'd many a plan;
But beware left repentance too late caufe you pain,
And attend to the lefson I give in my ftrain.
    Spare a halfpenny &c.

3

Through woods and through wilds oft'aweary I roam,
Long abfent from parents, from friends and from home;
Though fad is my heart, and tho' fore are my feet,
Yet I fing on my way thus to all that I meet.
    Spare a halfpenny &c.

For the German Flute.

A poor little Gypſy I wander for-lorn, My fortune was told long be-fore I was born, So fortunes I tell, as for-ſaken I ſtray, And in ſearch of my love, I am loſt on my way: Spare a halfpenny, Spare a halfpenny, Spare a poor little Gypſy a Gypſy a halfpenny, Spare a poor little Gypſy a halfpenny.

2

I fear from this line you have been a ſad man,
And to harm us poor girls, have form'd many a plan;
But beware leſt repentance too late cauſe you pain,
And attend to the leſſon I give in my ſtrain.
    Spare a halfpenny &c.

3

Through woods and through wilds oft' aweary I roam,
Long abſent from parents from friends and from home;
Though t'rd is my heart, and tho' ſore are my feet,
Yet I ſing on my way thus to all that I meet.
    Spare a halfpenny &c.

www.ingramcontent.com/pod-product-compliance
Lightning Source LLC
Chambersburg PA
CBHW022124160426
43197CB00009B/1150